Chicago Cubs Trivia Quiz Book

Copyright 2013,
All rights reserved.

Published by Mega Media Depot
P.O. Box 945
Prospect Heights, Il 60070

Manufactured in the United States of America

Some of the images in this book are used under the terms of agreement and paid subscription plans with Clipart.com and Fotolia.com.

Disclaimer

IMPORTANT: All information in this book is for news matter and entertainment purposes only and is not intended to be used in any direct or indirect violation of local, state, federal or international law(s). Any use of information and recommendations provided by this book is to be used at a visitor's sole discretion. The author, owner and publisher are not liable for any losses or damages incurred directly or indirectly.

Were the Chicago Cubs founded in 1876?

No, the team was initially founded in 1870.

Were the Chicago Cubs initially named the Cubs?

No, the team actual was known as the Chicago White Stockings.

Was Albert Spalding, of Spalding Sporting Goods, a pitcher for the Chicago Cubs?

Yes, the founder of Spalding Sporting Goods was a pitcher for the Cubs going on to own the Cubs for a short while.

Have the Chicago Cubs ever won a World Series?

Yes, they won back-to-back World Series titles in 1907 and 1908.

Is the Chicago Cubs Wrigley stadium named after the chewing gum?

Chicago Cubs

Yes and No. The original field name was Weeghman Park but when Bill Wrigley, founder of Wrigley Gum, took part ownership, the field was renamed.

Are the Chicago Cubs cursed?

No,In 1945, a patron brought a billy goat to the Game 4 World Series game at Wrigley Field. P.K. Wrigley, owner at the time, ejected the patron and his goat when he uttered the words, "the Cubs, they ain't gonna win no more."

Were the Chicago Cubs ever known as "The Loveable Losers"?

Yes, during the 1970s this was the team's nickname.

Was Sammy Sosa the only Chicago Cubs player to hit a homerun in 5 straight games?

No, both Ryne Sandberg and Hack Wilson also hit a homerun in 5 straight games.

Chicago Cubs

Was it nearly four decades later when the Chicago Cubs won their division to advance to the playoffs?

Yes, the Cubs won their division in 1984 but failed to make it to the World Series.

Chicago Cubs

Was there ever a riot at Wrigley Field?

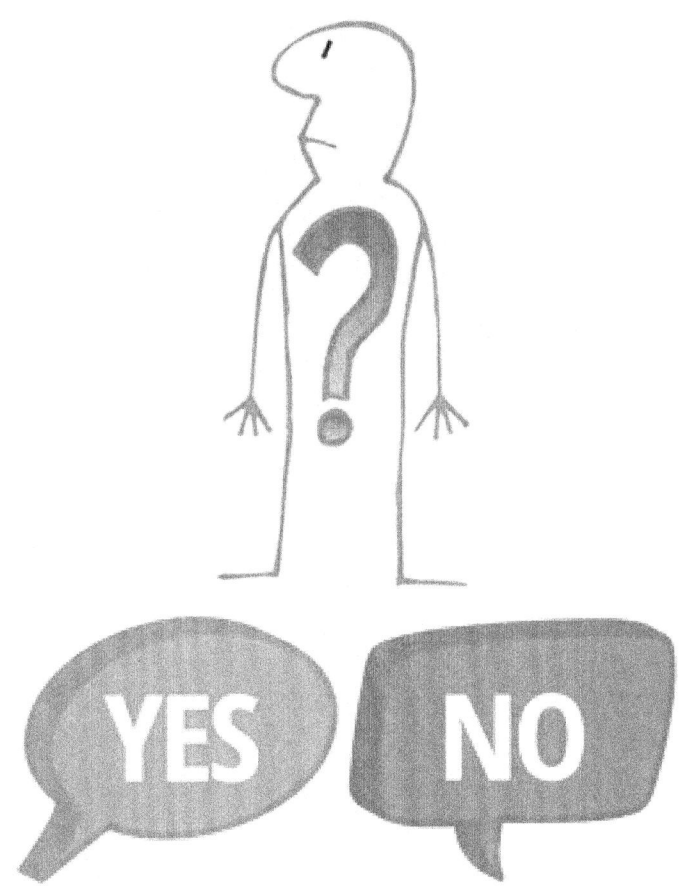

Yes, in 1928 nearly 5000 fans swarmed the field after a Chicago Cub player jumped into the stands to punch a heckling fan.

Does Chicago Cub player Hack Wilson have the record for most RBIs in a single season?

Chicago Cubs

Yes, he holds the record with 191 as of 2013.

Chicago Cubs

Was 1984 the last time the Cubs played in the World Series?

No, the last time the Chicago Cubs played in the World Series was 1945.

Is the Chicago Cubs curse known as "the curse of the billy goat"?

Chicago Cubs

Yes.

Is the Chicago Cubs spring training field called HoHoKam Park?

Yes, it is located in Mesa, Arizona.

Was Harry Caray a radio announcer for the Chicago Cubs?

Yes, for 17 years retiring in 1997.

Chicago Cubs

Are the Chicago Cubs are still owned by the Wrigley family?

No, as of 2009 the Ricketts family owns the team. Joe Ricketts is the founder of TD Ameritrade.

Did the Chicago Tribune ever own the Chicago Cubs?

Chicago Cubs

Yes, from 1981 to 2007.

Does "white flag time at Wrigley" mean that the Chicago Cubs won their game that day?

Yes, broadcaster Chip Caray coined it.

Chicago Cubs

Did the Chicago Cubs retire Greg Maddux's number?

Chicago Cubs

Yes, his number was retired.

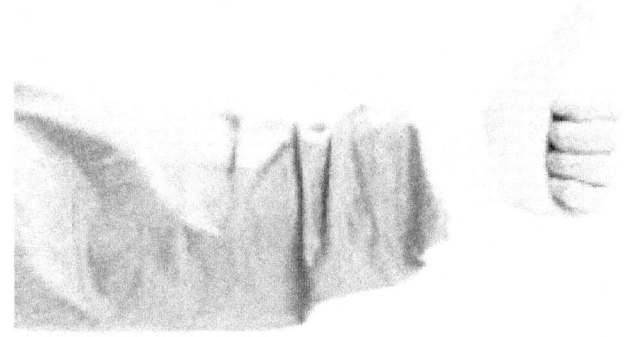

Are the Chicago Cubs also known as the Cubbies?

Chicago Cubs

Yes, that is another nickname associated to the Chicago Cubs.

CPSIA information can be obtained
at www.ICGtesting.com
Printed in the USA
LVOW13s0236130717
541181LV00006B/300/P